MAKE TODAY MATTER

Other Books by Chris Lowney

Pope Francis: Why He Leads the Way He Leads
(Loyola Press)

*Heroic Leadership: Best Practices from a 450-Year-Old
Company That Changed the World* (Loyola Press)

*Heroic Living: Discover Your Purpose and
Change the World* (Loyola Press)

*A Vanished World: Muslims, Christians, and Jews in
Medieval Spain* (Oxford University Press)

Guide to the Camino Ignaciano (with José Luis
Iriberri, SJ, coauthor) (Grupo de
Comunicación Loyola)

Everyone Leads: How to Revitalize the Catholic Church
(Rowman & Littlefield)

MAKE TODAY MATTER

10 HABITS
for a
BETTER LIFE
(and World)

CHRIS LOWNEY

LOYOLA PRESS.
A JESUIT MINISTRY
Chicago

LOYOLA PRESS.
A JESUIT MINISTRY

3441 N. Ashland Avenue
Chicago, Illinois 60657
(800) 621-1008
www.loyolapress.com

Portions of this book first appeared in *Heroic Living: Discover Your Purpose and Change the World*, by Chris Lowney (Chicago: Loyola Press, 2009).

Scripture quotations are from the *New Revised Standard Version Bible: Catholic Edition*, copyright 1989, 1993, Division of Christian Education of the National Council of the Churches of Christ in the United States of America. Used by permission. All rights reserved.

Cover art credit: Loyola Press

ISBN: 978-0-8294-4663-0
Library of Congress Control Number: 2017963072

Printed in the United States of America.
18 19 20 21 22 23 24 25 26 27 28 Versa 10 9 8 7 6 5 4 3 2 1

Contents

Why Does It Take a Crisis?

Picture Houston in the aftermath of Hurricane Harvey's fury: Streets are flooded, and fetid water is rising in countless houses. Cell-phone coverage is spotty. Downed power lines have cast swaths of a vibrant city into darkness.

Now picture Larry, a friend of mine, who struggles through that chaos to reach his elderly, infirm parents in their flooded home: "We used a raft to evacuate my mother, who is bedbound with Parkinson's disease, and steadied my father as he used his walker to make the block-long journey through four-foot flood waters."

Those anguished images of his parents remain seared in his memory. But something else struck him even more powerfully. "Chris, the remarkable part was the cooperation, support, and mercy that was shown by so many, like the stranger who literally seemed to show up out of nowhere with the raft that saved my mother. There was no racial tension, no political discord, no infighting. . . . It was a city in which people needed and were given so much support and help."

Few will be surprised that these Houstonians rose to the occasion and bonded to support one another. Crises often bring out the best in people. Ordinary persons become selfless heroes in the wake of disaster.

At such moments, we are no longer irked by life's minor annoyances; our sense of what ultimately matters becomes more vivid; we want to be our very best selves; we're energized to make some positive difference.

But why does it take a crisis to bring out our very best? Why not rise to the occasion every single day?

My friend Paul manages to do just that. A vibrant, young father of two sons and principal breadwinner for his family, he had been sledge-hammered with an unexpected cancer diagnosis and given a few months to live.

That was years ago. A treatment regimen transformed his death sentence into a chronic but manageable medical condition. Still, that experience of impending death transformed his attitude toward life. He tells me that, ever since that time, "There's no such thing as a bad day." He's grateful every morning. He takes nothing for granted. He makes every day count.

He does many of the same things he always did, the same things we all do: goes for walks, phones his wife during the day, drives his kids to appointments, has dinner with friends, and goes to work every day. For most of us, such ordinary moments seem inconsequential; we drift through them, half distracted by something else on a to-do list. We typically forget them by the next morning.

But, for Paul? He's more present during these small moments. His mind no longer strays in the hinterlands of regrets and dreams. Instead of surrendering to apathy or crankiness, he approaches each day with determination and gratitude.

He seizes each day as a unique opportunity, because he sees each day as a gift. Which is exactly what this book is about: seizing today's opportunity, and rising to the occasion every single day.

If even a few million more of us could live with such focus and a strong sense of purpose, we would transform this world into a kinder, more loving, and more just home.

I know it's not that simple. Each morning, we're swept anew into the chaotic maelstrom of career, social media, and consumerism. I focus on my to-do list and lose track of the big questions: *Why am I doing this, anyway? What ultimately matters?* That's why the following chapter will invite us to revisit the big questions and to declare what matters.

Yet, it's one thing to declare what matters, quite another to do what matters every single day. It's been far easier for me to envision my ideal self than to become that ideal self. For example, I wasn't quite brave enough to say what needed to be said in that meeting; wasn't empathetic enough to offer the help that stranger obviously needed; haven't mustered the fierce willpower to keep developing my gifts; or don't dare to chase that dream of a new career direction. I've let too many hours slip away, distracted by a social media feed instead of pursuing a dozen more important pursuits.

I can do better; we all can do better. I know that, because I've been inspired over the years by ordinary folks who have excelled at making every day matter. They are neither superhuman nor saints (well, at least one of them might be—read on). But they model attitudes and habits that turn them into happier, more grateful, and more effective people. The practices they cultivate are simple: Any one of us could emulate them tomorrow. Let's start. Let's hear their stories, and let's explore how we can do the same.

First Things First: Decide What Matters

"If, like archers, we have a target to aim at, we are more likely to hit the right mark."

Aristotle said that. Aristotle was wrong.

Far be it from me to second-guess one of humanity's intellectual heavyweights. But how I wish my life were as straightforward as target practice with a bow and arrow. Life is like aiming at a moving target while riding a horse. Oh, and while I'm shooting arrows at the target, someone else is shooting arrows at me.

Aristotle wasn't talking about archery or even about life "targets" such as a great job, a nicer home, or getting tonight's dinner onto the table. He was speaking of more fundamental concerns, such as what a happy, purposeful life entails. Or, what really matters.

And he has a point: You'll never hit a target that you don't see, and most of us don't keep our target clearly enough in view. Who hops out of bed each morning thinking, *Lo and behold! My life target lies clearly before me! Let me devote this new day to hitting my target.*

The Roman philosopher Seneca had his own take on that idea: "If one does not know to what port one is sailing, no wind is favorable."

Without a clear vision of what makes life meaningful, one can end up adrift.

I once heard a story about a phenomenally successful business entrepreneur who started suffering the doubts that sometimes afflict phenomenally successful people. Once they reach the top, they wonder, *Is this all there is?*

It's understandable. Driven people sometimes get to the top by focusing almost maniacally on, well, getting to the top. They lead blinkered lives. Even family life gets pushed to the periphery. They keep hitting one professional target after another, all the way up the ladder. Until they reach the top and wonder if they're on the wrong ladder after all.

So this entrepreneur sought out someone who really did seem to have life figured out: Mother Teresa of Calcutta, world renowned for humble service to the world's poorest folks. She radiated the serenity and sure sense of purpose that he craved.

So he left his fashionable New York neighborhood for Mother Teresa's unfashionable Calcutta neighborhood. But getting there was only half his challenge. See, Mother Teresa wasn't very interested in chatting with rich guys about the meaning of life. Her priority was tending to Calcutta's destitute and dying. But the businessman persisted, and Mother Teresa made time for what he assumed would be the first of many deep conversations.

He explained that he'd come to begin a dialogue with her about the keys to a meaningful life. He asked if she had any preliminary wisdom to share. She simply said, "Pray every day, and never do anything that you know is wrong."

Then she just looked at him, I would like to imagine in a kindly way, but also in a way that probably implied, *Okay? I gave you your answer. Are we finished now? I have things to do.*

The guy must have sat there for a moment, jet-lagged and dumbfounded. But give him credit for realizing, *What can I say to that?* He stood up, thanked her, and went back home. Whether he followed her advice, I can't say.

But Mother Teresa was implicitly challenging us (and him) to reorder priorities as we consider the targets we aim for. That is, instead of thinking first about a career or financial goal, decide first what kind of person you want to become. Only when your vision of what ultimately matters is clear in your mind are you in a position to make good choices about career, lifestyle, and so on. As for the inner peace and sense of meaning that this entrepreneur (and each of us) craves, those won't flow from what we have and earn but from how we live and relate to fellow humans.

So, what matters? I've read dense tomes about that question over the years, but I always find myself pulled back to some simple ideas. Taken together, those ideas coalesce into a target of sorts, a picture of the kind of person I want to be. Here are a few of the ideas that have become important to me.

- To give as much love as I have received
- "Whatever you did for one of the least brothers [and sisters] of mine, you did for me." (Jesus of Nazareth)
- "What does the Lord require of you but to do justice, and to love kindness, and to walk humbly with your God."
- Do to no one what you yourself hate.
- Spread love everywhere you go. Let no one come to you without leaving happier.

I'd be awfully happy if I became worthy of an epitaph like "Here lies Chris, who gave as much love as he received, and who never did to anyone else what he himself hated" and so on. I'm still a very long way from getting there, but I know where I want to go.

Make It Personal

How about you? How do you want to live? What's your target? What ideas do you keep coming back to, whether for reassurance that you haven't lost your way or for direction to get back on track?

Why not put this book aside, take twenty minutes, and answer some of those questions? Yes, right now. Keep your answers to one page, max, and keep that page in an accessible place in case any refinements cross your mind as you continue this book.

Then, stick the page in your Bible, day planner, cookbook, or whatever book you open regularly. At least a few times each year, review these thoughts about what matters.

I wish I could assure you that, once you know how you want to live, you will always live that way. If only it were that simple. I fall short of my aspirations pretty regularly, for lots of reasons. Yet all those reasons relate to a simple fact: I'm human, and if you didn't know, *human* is the Latin word for "screws things up on a daily basis." Here's how the great Christian apostle Paul summed up his own shortcomings and the human condition: "For I do not do what I want, but I do the very thing I hate."

My problem has not been figuring out how I want to live; my problem has been living that way. My ideas about what matters aren't complicated; it's just that I'm complicated and the world is complicated.

Some years back, I helped care for my mother as she slowly slid toward death from leukemia. Talk about hitting the target—I've never felt so certain that I was doing what mattered. I loved my mother and felt so blessed to help support her.

Yet, even though my purpose was supremely worthy, my daily behavior was sometimes less admirable. I was sleep deprived, frightened, and stressed, and it showed: I sometimes snapped at a visiting nurse, lost my temper with the insurance company's call-center staff, or became defensive if my siblings asked about reconsidering some decision I had made.

But at least I was pursuing a supremely worthy purpose during those months, which is more than I can say about other life episodes, when I was temporarily pulled off course by selfishness, greed, laziness, anger, lust (let's not forget that one), or a dozen other inner demons.

The remedy was not to rethink my long-term vision of what matters; rather, I simply needed to pay more attention to the short term, to whatever crazy impulses were leading me astray. The following chapters will help us to do just that: pay more attention, every day; we'll acquire habits that help us to pursue what matters.

Such habits have never been more essential. It was challenging enough to tame our inner demons and keep our priorities in order; now we must do so amidst a world that grows devilishly complex and volatile.

When taking care of my mother, for example, I was constantly thrust into situations for which I felt utterly unprepared: processing complicated medical data, treatment options, insurance regulations, you name it. And as I struggled to reach decisions about her care, all the circumstances seemed in flux: an infection would creep in, or her temperature would spike. It felt as if some perverse goblin took delight in yanking the rug from under me every time I had found my footing.

The military world has a term for that—*VUCA*: "volatile, uncertain, confusing, and ambiguous." The acronym describes the fog of war, where soldiers must make decisions under the worst possible conditions.

Well, I hope no one is shooting bullets at you, but you, too, are coping with volatility, uncertainty, confusion, and ambiguity as you accompany a loved one through serious illness, raise a teenager, decide which of a hundred different career paths to follow, deal with a substance-abusing friend, or decide what's ethical when virtually every behavior short of murder seems acceptable to someone nowadays.

Marry our VUCA world to our human frailties, and hitting one's target in life can feel like a ten-meter high dive into a backyard kiddie pool.

I opened this chapter by comparing twenty-first-century life to hitting a moving target. But I realize that I had it backwards: The target isn't moving; everything else is. The target is often clear enough: Most of us know what matters to us. We want to be happy, make a positive difference, and make the world a bit better.

I can see the port I want to reach, as Seneca put it; I can envision what kind of person I want to be. And sometimes the life journey seems easy: calm seas and wind at my back. Other times are difficult and even frightening: Storms arise; I get blown off course; and my compass breaks.

At such times I'm reminded of that famous fisherman's prayer: "Oh God, thy sea is so vast and my boat is so small." Life sometimes feels that way in today's VUCA world. But people successfully navigate its complexity all the time. We meet some of these people in the chapters to follow.

Habit 1—Point Out the Way

My high-school homeroom teacher lured freshmen into gambling. Sort of.

Father Steve Duffy would roam the school cafeteria, inducing gullible teens to allocate some of their lunch money to his football betting pool. Each week's winner took home half the proceeds; Duffy sent the rest to impoverished communities overseas.

He pursued other dubious pursuits too, such as scouring New York City streets for advertising posters that might enliven one of his classes. When he found a suitable poster, I guess he stole it. He told us that he asked permission, but I'm not sure he bothered. People were shooting each other on New York streets back then; who was going to arrest an old man in a priest outfit for pinching a cardboard advertisement?

Duffy ended up teaching at that high school for fifty-seven years; if that's not a record, it must be close. I met him when I was fourteen, about halfway through his career. Neither I nor any of my classmates would have bet that this gaunt, stoop-shouldered old priest would live for another ten years, much less teach for another twenty.

Still, while he looked like a stern-faced, crabby Old Testament prophet whenever he pointed one of his bony fingers, he turned out to be kind and nurturing. He taught Latin's unchanging conjugations without ever seeming bored. He invented kooky jingles and rhymes to help us memorize declensions, and he devoted his after-school hours to tutoring the kids who were falling behind.

He also taught religion, startling us freshmen with his appalling rendition of a *Porgy and Bess* song: "the things that you're liable to read in the Bible, they ain't necessarily so." It was shocking to hear a priest say so, but that's how Duffy taught us that biblical passages must often be interpreted rather than read literally, because Scripture's divinely-inspired truths are sometimes conveyed through poetry or storytelling.

Even though that was sophisticated stuff for a high schooler, Duffy's religion classes were easy because he handed out custom-made summaries of each lesson. Even kids who floundered in Latin could salvage self-esteem with an A in religion. In fact, by senior year, Duffy himself seemed too easy. His antics seemed better suited to high-school freshmen than to us eighteen-year-old sophisticates.

A few years later, while studying an advanced textbook on the Old Testament, I learned who had truly been sophisticated back in high school. As I read through the material, déjà vu plagued me. Chapter after chapter in that university book felt so familiar. I tracked down Duffy's mimeographed notes from a pack-rat friend who had saved his high-school religion notebook. Sure enough, the parallels were unmistakable. Duffy's handouts were based on a college textbook. He had taught college-level theology to fourteen-year-olds and made the material seem easy.

But only years later did I understand what Duffy was really teaching. Someone had cajoled him into articulating his teaching philosophy, and he published a short essay about his approach to students: "I see myself radiating Christ to my students at all times. . . . I do this by my concern and love and respect for them. . . . I do it by being friendly in my dealings with them . . . [I think of Jesus] traveling with his companions, being with them twenty-four hours a day, and always having an effect on them by the way he dealt with them."

Duffy's point is relevant, whether you're a Christian or not, whether you are a teacher, parent, or corporate executive. You may not think of yourself radiating Christ to those around you, but you're radiating something all the time: kindness or meanness, curiosity or closed-mindedness, respect or disregard. As the Presbyterian minister Frederick Buechner once put it, "It is not so much their subjects that the great teachers teach as it is themselves." So it is: I barely remember any Latin, but I sure do remember Duffy's creative spirit and the way he treated me.

Like Duffy, I taught high school, but only for a couple of years. Unlike Duffy, I thought I was there primarily to teach economics. (Supply and demand curves, anyone?) Once kids understood, say, the equation we were studying, I ticked it off my to-do list and moved on to the next lesson. I see now that I didn't quite get it. The lessons don't end when the class or meeting does. We are always making an impact—in the case of the teacher, outside class as well as in the class; in the case of office workers, during every passing encounter with colleagues. What Duffy observed about Jesus is true for the rest of us as well: We are "always having an effect on [others] by the way [we deal] with them."

I use a straightforward dictionary definition of leadership when I conduct workshops: Leadership is the ability "to point out a way, direction or goal . . . and to influence others toward it." Isn't it true that each of us is leading in one way or another all the time? Parents are "pointing out a way" for their children when they model virtues such as patience, discipline, or fairness—or, unfortunately, when they model racism or greed or self-centeredness. We can lead for good or for ill. Students point out a way when they model hard work and a commitment to personal growth. As the great humanitarian Albert Schweitzer put it, "Example is not the main thing in influencing others. It is the only thing."

I doubt Duffy ever thought of himself as a leader, but he embodied that word. He knew what "way" he wanted to point out: "concern and love and respect." And he knew that he was always influencing others, making an impact by his presence and behavior.

Maybe you don't think of yourself as a leader. It's time to start. You are, in fact, leading, well or poorly, all the time, by the influence you are having, first on your family, then on friends and neighbors, on colleagues at work, or on customers, students, teammates, patients, whatever the case may be.

Leadership is not some destination you may reach if you become company president, school principal, or head nurse. Rather, leadership is happening every day, because you're influencing everyone around you. It's time to make the most out of this opportunity.

Make It Personal

If an objective observer shadowed you for a week, what "way"—that is, what priorities and values—would they say you are modeling?

Recall at least three situations in the last week where you may have influenced someone by your example.

Habit 2—Bring Big Heart Every Day

Some years ago, I attempted the five-hundred-mile pilgrim trek to Santiago de Compostela, where the relics of St. James the apostle are honored. Type A personality that I am, I prepared well in advance, striding New York City streets for hours, lugging a backpack weighted with phone books (remember paper phone books?).

But within a week of starting the trek itself, I wasn't striding but hobbling. I didn't blame God for my two badly blistered heels, just the sort of bad luck that can afflict anyone, as I've seen many times since while leading group treks along another pilgrim route I heartily recommend, the Ignatian Camino. (Look it up!)

Anyway, I tried to persevere. After slowly shuffling into a small village one afternoon, I recognized a fellow pilgrim with whom I had crossed paths a few days earlier. She was standing at a bus stop, her backpack at her feet. I tottered over for a chat. She had given up. She was grabbing the next bus to start the journey home. Her body hadn't faltered; her will had.

She shrugged, smiled ruefully, and looked at me. "If I had your heart and my feet, I could walk to the end of the world."

It was one of the best compliments I've ever received.

Before you conclude that this chapter will be a "look at me" production, know this: I'm not really that guy, the iron-willed enthusiast who brings big heart all the time. But I was that guy during the trek, even though I, too, eventually dropped out, on a doctor's recommendation. It barely disappointed me that I hadn't made it all the way to Santiago. I knew I had given it my all, and that was all the satisfaction I needed.

Upon returning to New York, I got in touch with yet another pilgrim, who, unlike me, had barreled through Spain like Robo-pilgrim. While blistered feet kept curtailing my daily distances, he felt strong and soon left me behind, pushing himself to longer distances each day, exploring his potential.

But returning to work had left him unsettled, and he later e-mailed me words to this effect: "Out on the camino, I saw how much I was capable of. Now back here, to put it in camino terms, I see that I've been content to go ten miles each day, when I'm capable of so much more. There's lots for me to think about."

There was lots for me to think about too. I've mentioned that I once taught economics. After a couple years of those same old supply-demand curves, I became bored. I sometimes wondered why old Duffy had never become bored by Latin's unchanging conjugations.

Eventually I got it: Of course, he must have been bored sometimes, or fed up with kids who didn't try hard. He was human, subject to the same frustrations that plague any of us, whether we're doing family laundry, raising surly teenagers, or analyzing corporate tax returns.

But whereas I reacted by "mailing it in" sometimes and settling for good-enough work, "good enough" didn't cut it for Duffy, who prowled subway cars in imaginative pursuit of that extra touch that might spark a student's imagination and intelligence. He embodied a quote from St. Augustine: "I will suggest a means whereby you can praise God all day long, if you wish. Whatever you do, do it well, and you have praised God." Augustine was likely riffing on Ecclesiastes: "Whatever your hand finds to do, do it with your might."

I sure did what Ecclesiastes counseled during that trek across Spain but not always while teaching in that school. So, go to school on me. Heed Ecclesiastes, or, more colloquially, bring big heart every day.

If you don't, you might end up unhappy. That's how the renowned late psychologist Abraham Maslow saw it: "If you plan on being anything less than you are capable of being, you will probably be unhappy."

What's more, if you live with bighearted spirit, you just might infect some of us with it too. Think of my old teacher Duffy. His commitment to excellence, for example, kindled his absurd belief that fourteen-year-olds could digest college-level theology if it was fed to them appropriately. His excellence coaxed our minds to blossom. The Latin root of *excel* conveys the sense of rising out of or rising above. That's what excellence is: rising above ourselves and lifting up those around us.

A former business colleague of mine had once coached track. Right before a race, he would get into his runner's face, lock eyes with the athlete, and whisper, "You're going to run this race like it's the last race you'll ever run in your life."

It was a motivational technique but not a manipulative one. Today could be the "last race"—lives can be transformed in an instant by heart attacks or car accidents. But we can make the most of today's opportunity, whether it's a work challenge, a conversation, a workout, or a daily prayer; we don't know how many more will come our way.

Don't interpret that coach's maxim as relevant only for peak moments, such as a job interview, a marriage proposal, or a final exam. Rather, that exhortation ought to become a lifelong attitude toward your many gifts. You've been entrusted with a treasure, blessed with so many gifts, talents, resources, and opportunities.

I don't mean *gifts* and *talents* in some small-minded, worldly sense. I can't dunk basketballs or finesse Mozart piano concertos, for example—most of us can't. But we have some smarts, energy, free time, spare change, a social network, the world's accumulated knowledge on our smartphones, and a touch of wisdom that we've gathered over the years.

Recently I was chatting with a friend, a high-school president; Margaret had just happened across one of her students, whose beautiful black hair hung almost to her waist. "Wow," my friend said, "your hair is so beautiful; you're growing it so long!"

"Yes," the student replied. "I want to grow it even a bit longer; then I'm going to donate it to be made into hairpieces for people who have lost their hair because of sickness."

Margaret turned to me. "I was bowled over. I was so inspired. What put such an idea into this young person's heart?"

Even my *hair* as a gift, a talent, an opportunity? Well, not my hair, I assure you. But maybe for some of us, at some moments.

That student, my *camino* experience, psychologist Maslow, and Duffy the teacher all underscore the same lesson. Bring big heart by making the most of every opportunity, by perceiving your opportunities as broadly as you can, and by developing your gifts as fully as you can, and using your gifts for great purposes. And do all of that every day, whether studying Latin, teaching kids, managing coworkers, or pursuing manifold other opportunities. Lift up yourself and the rest of us, just as Duffy's commitment to excellence helped his students become more excellent themselves.

It turned out that I didn't have the feet to walk across Spain, at least that year. But I had the heart to do so, and fullhearted commitment, I can report, brings its own deep happiness and satisfaction.

Run every race as if it's your last, so that afterwards you can look in a mirror and say, "I put my heart into it, and I used my gifts to my utmost, and for purposes I can feel proud of."

Make It Personal

Think of two or three moments in which you "brought big heart," whether in caring for your family, working at your job, or developing your gifts. In what other aspect of life do you want to begin bringing that same spirit?

The root of the word *excellence* connotes rising above ourselves and inspiring others to do so. What opportunities will you have in the next month to inspire others to rise above themselves?

Habit 3—Don't Win the Race:
Contribute to the (Human) Race

Run this race as if it's the last one of your life. Hard work beats talent that won't work hard.

Sports coaches coined such phrases to motivate athletes to thump their competitors.

That's precisely why those sayings, while great in sports arenas, aren't perfect proverbs for life. We can take them as an attitude about our talent but not about how we should treat fellow human beings. A meaningful life entails doing your best with your talent, not getting the best of another person.

Forgetting that difference is a first step toward a bitter life. Remember Maslow's saying about not knowing many happy people who haven't used their talents well? Well, I don't know many happy people whose lives are all about winning, either—though, don't get me wrong, winning is fun.

Each of us needs to decide, *Is my life about whom I will beat, or about whom I will be? Am I here on earth to contribute to some worthy purpose, or to race against other people?* When my life is about contributing, I rise above myself. When life is about comparing myself to others, I descend into the bottomless pit of ego needs.

Take it from me. I worked in a profession renowned for big egos. For example, let me describe what bonus day was like for a managing director of a major investment bank. I would meet one-on-one with each of my subordinates, meeting after meeting, all day long. I would thank each one for the hard work and sacrifices during the year. None of them heard that because they listened only for the big reveal: What is my bonus for this year? I would cut to the chase pretty quickly, reveal the bonus number, and explain why management colleagues and I thought it appropriate.

Many were gracious. Once, an overjoyed subordinate jumped up and gave me a big hug. But others would remain poker-faced, even grim. Poker-faced: *Gee, that's more than I thought he would pay me! But if I let that show, he might skimp on my bonus next year.* Grim: *I bet this guy is screwing me in comparison to my peers.*

Mind you, these bonuses were not like a fifteen percent tip on top of a fifty-dollar restaurant tab. These bonuses often far exceeded the average American's annual earnings, on top of an already generous salary.

At least once I watched a crying multimillionaire explain why his bonus was unfair. Here's how a partner in a rival firm once described the bonus-day demeanor of investment bankers: "They are either sullen or mutinous but never quite happy."

Imagine how the tension would build all day as each sullen banker slunk back to his desk, then gossiped with colleagues about the bonuses of internal rivals. Imagine my own tension. For, even while placating the crybabies, I was anxiously awaiting my boss's summons to my own "big reveal." I always thanked my boss and acknowledged how much money it was. But even when pleasantly surprised, I never brought myself to exclaim, "Wow! That's more than I imagined! You made my day." I guess I didn't want to give my boss any reason to skimp on me next year either.

How could the planet's best-paid people succumb to such behavior? Instead of bitching about why we deserved more, we should have been cartwheeling through J. P. Morgan's hallways, then falling to our knees in gratitude for our undeserved good fortune, then joyfully hatching schemes to donate our excess to others.

Yes, it was undeserved good fortune. We weren't paid so well because we were better than everyone else. A hundred million more-talented people across the world probably could have outperformed us if given the same opportunities. But they had lost the birth lottery: born poor in underdeveloped countries that lacked great education systems, good healthcare, political stability, and well-paying industries. We, in contrast, had been blessed with all those privileges; we had been born on third base yet somehow convinced ourselves that we had hit triples.

But our self-congratulatory chest-thumping never brought lasting peace or inner satisfaction. When our lives revolve around comparing ourselves to others, we will always compare unfavorably to someone, somewhere. Every banker would end up suspecting that he or she had been paid less than some internal rival. That's what galled the sullen or mutinous, who would protest that "it isn't about the money." It was about what they called "fairness" or "keeping score" or "being the best." Give them credit for honesty if not for insight, because "keeping score" was exactly what it was about.

In investment banking, we kept score by money. In high school, we kept score by our relative popularity. Midlife crises descend, and we keep score by comparing summer homes or facial wrinkles. The "am I winning" disease afflicts us at every age and in whatever we're doing.

For example, after I left the investment banking industry, grateful (truly) for all I had received, I started writing books. Authors earn nothing unless writing zombie fiction or diet guides. Surely, then, laborers in the noble literary vineyard are doing it for love and are immune to the "am I winning" virus?

Think again. A publisher once invited me to co-headline a leadership conference in Colombia with Ken Blanchard, the legendary guru who coauthored *The One Minute Manager*. I use the word *co-headline* loosely. Blanchard was like U2, and I was like the obscure opening band that plays while folks are still settling into their seats. Still, it was heady stuff, complete with a private plane ride and an enormous, packed venue.

A book signing followed the conference, where I savored the giddy ego rush of feeling my wrist grow numb as the long line of book buyers snaked forward for my signature. Then I made a big mistake: I glanced across the room. Blanchard's line was so much longer that it must have stretched to the Venezuelan border. My ego high temporarily evaporated;

I was envious. But even while it happened, I knew how pathetic it all was. I shook my head, nearly laughed out loud, and went back to signing books.

Any one of us can fall prey to the affliction of comparing ourselves to others. If it's not about money or fame, it might be better clothes, a cooler car, bigger houses, better looks, newer kitchen appliances, more friends on Facebook, more "likes" for our posts, the schools our kids get into, who got the lead role in the play, or a thousand other things.

Trouble is, we can never win the game of "am I winning." My bonus will always be smaller than someone's, and someone else will always sell more books or have a nicer kitchen, more friends, or cooler parties. No matter what I accumulate, I'll still find someone with more.

We in the developed world are healthier and more prosperous than any civilization in history, but we're still vaguely dissatisfied and chasing something that always tantalizingly eludes us. When asked, for example, how much annual income they would need to "live well," Americans at virtually every income level answer, "Twice as much."

This means that the person earning $50,000 annually believes he or she needs $100,000 to live well, and those making $200,000 believe they need $400,000, and so on up the ladder. The exhausting chase is driving us all nuts; we've forgotten the plain wisdom attributed to second-century Rabbi Meir: "Who is truly wealthy? Those who are content with what they have."

Only one cure exists for the "am I winning" virus: Don't treat your life as a race to be won. Don't focus on getting to the top of the heap, because every peak you reach will yield a clearer view of the next summit, already occupied by another competitor in the game of life.

Run every race as if it's your last, but decide first why you're running. Instead of competing against me or anyone else, why not contribute your energies to making us better people, through your coaching, love, inspiring example, or noble mission? Instead of trying to win the race, why not make it your mission to contribute to the race, the *human* race—by making your corner of the world more just, more loving, and more happy.

Make It Personal

When are you most likely to feel as if you're in competition with others rather than in partnership with them?

In what ways do you contribute to some cause greater than yourself and your interests?

Habit 4—Give Away Your Sneakers: Help Someone Today

Be like the guy who crossed the parking lot with no shoes.

I chair the board of one of America's largest hospital systems, and each year we publish what we call "sacred stories" that epitomize why we're doing what we're doing. Yes, we're patching up broken bones and leaky hearts, but, above all, we exist to reverence our fellow humans: That's one of our core values. The Collins dictionary tells us that reverence is "a feeling or attitude of deep respect, love, and awe, as for something sacred." Anyone who has held a newborn baby or a dying relative's hand can relate to that feeling of reverence, and our health system wants everyone who enters our care to be treated with exactly that spirit, even in a frenzied emergency room, which was the setting for a short sacred story that deeply impressed me.

"One night in June, we saw one of our routine patients, who was without shoes. He was also homeless. When the patient was ready to be discharged from the emergency department, Dr. Hughes took off his shoes and gave them to the patient. The patient was appreciative, and Dr. Hughes left for home without shoes."

This happened in Durango, Colorado, a picturesque town perched so high in the Rockies that temperatures may well have fallen into the thirties on that June evening. Dr. Hughes's shoeless stroll to his car might have been nippy. But his was a short commute home to a closet filled with shoes, compared with the prospect of sending a barefoot, homeless guy back onto the streets.

When I tracked down the doctor to talk with him about this, he brushed off his act of kindness. When the guy said he needed shoes, the doctor said, "without much thought, I looked at my worn-out, old running shoes, and handed them to the patient. . . . I really don't consider it a sacrifice at all. These shoes had already put on many miles."

He just did what any of us would do, right? Except that we don't always do it when the moment comes. We're too busy, rushed, or distracted to notice some passing chance to do good.

Or, we do notice, but some inner demon—a fear, an insecurity, a bad habit—holds us back. A friend once lived in a country where street beggars were common. Whenever her husband was approached for money, he cheerfully fished a coin from his pocket for the beggar, and then for the next beggar, and for the one after that.

The wife said something like this: "Chris, I envy him, because I reach into my pocketbook and take out a coin, and I really want to give, but then it's as if a string is attached to my hand, and I think of some reason not to give."

I know all about that string. It often holds me back too. I don't want to give money to someone who may spend it on drugs; I'm too rushed to chat with the elderly neighbor in my building lobby; I don't pick up that piece of trash on the street because it won't make much difference. Taken alone, such moments seem insignificant.

But what if we did the right thing, even part of the time? Think of thousands of such moments across my lifetime, and thousands more across yours, not to mention the lost chances of seven billion more people on earth. Those missed chances are the difference between the hurting planet we have and the just, loving planet that we all wish we had.

When I was a Jesuit trainee, I was encouraged to read biographies of Jesuit saints. Many of these books were dreadful, written decades ago in a pietistic, schmaltzy style that did no justice to their heroic subjects. But I remember one story I hope is true, about St. Robert Bellarmine, a renowned theologian and cardinal.

Beggars would call at his episcopal residence, and he always surrendered a couple of coins or a candlestick or some small furnishing. As his residence slowly emptied of accoutrements, a friend chided Bellarmine's naïveté: "You're being duped; charlatans are showing up and ripping you off." Bellarmine supposedly replied that he would rather be taken advantage of a hundred times than send away one needy person.

Do something good today. Don't judge others; just act. That was Bellarmine's attitude, and so, too, that of the doctor who gave away his sneakers. As a small-town emergency-room doctor, he recognized that homeless person as a frequent ER visitor. Dr. Hughes suffered no illusion that his sneakers would be the man's first step toward responsible sobriety. Rather, as he confessed to me, he sometimes felt "annoyed at having done all my years of medical training just to be a doctor for drunks." So he sometimes had to fight against his initial response. "My natural inclination—and my wife can attest to this—is to take the easy way out and help someone out only when it is convenient."

His "natural inclination" to take the easy way out is like that little string that prevents my friend from handing a coin to the beggar. Everyone suffers those moments when we let a broken piece of us get the better of us, so everyone needs a way to get over them. Dr. Hughes does so, he told me, by challenging himself: *What would the Lord do in my place?* That three-second mental break pulls him out of the daily fray and reminds him of what matters. Then he gets back into the game and gets on with the day.

Each day presents opportunities to do good for another, to give away your sneakers, so to speak. Don't let those opportunities slip by. Free yourself from the inclination to walk on by, to judge others as unworthy of help, or from anything else that holds you back from making every day count.

Make It Personal

Call to mind one instance in the past week when you "gave away your sneakers," so to speak.

Call to mind an instance in the past week when you walked by an opportunity to "give away your sneakers" and enter someone's small moment of need, whether for conversation, material help, compassion, or merely for accompaniment.

Habit 5—Banish the Inner Demons: Be Free for What Matters

I remember when the moving van delivered three decades' and three continents' worth of my accumulated junk to the apartment I now share with my wife: small boxes of books; taller, wardrobe-style boxes of hanging clothes; and oddly shaped boxes that cradled mementos such as a windup Victrola from the 1920s or a ceramic plate bought in Ürümqi, China.

I pried open each box and presented to my wife the flotsam and jetsam of my bachelorhood. She sometimes gave a thumbs up; more often, though, she grimly shook her head no. I dutifully added each reject to a rapidly mounting donate-to-Salvation-Army pile (well, I hid a few things from her; don't tell). For the first hour or so of this traumatic ritual,

I suppressed some irritation. *Jettison the Chairman Mao 1995 calendar purchased in a Beijing flea market? Really?* After an hour, my annoyance yielded to a vaguely resentful sigh of resignation, and I just got on with it.

Now, a few years later? I don't even remember half that stuff and can't imagine why it had seemed important to me at the time. Getting rid of it has lightened my load and freed me, in some small way, for the shared journey of married life.

Picture the alternative: my wife and me on a new journey together, me straining to keep up while dragging along a shipping container crammed with the Mao calendar, the books I no longer read, the saggy jeans I liked to wear, and whatnot. I wasn't going to run each race as if it were my last while wearing those saggy jeans and lugging all that junk.

I had also collected habits over the years, such as reserving Sunday mornings for newspaper reading, or eating dinner at a certain time, and plenty of others. Some of those had to go too. Nothing wrong with any of those habits, mind you, or with collecting souvenirs or liking comfortable old clothes.

But think of all that as metaphor for the internal stuff that could have held me back from investing fully in a shared life with my wife. To be sufficiently free for our new adventure, I had to relinquish not only my physical "stuff" but also my old habits, the ways I had done things over the years.

I had to become free from that inner baggage to be free for a higher purpose: a good marriage. Each of us needs the freedom to pursue what matters. But to get free, we have to give up the baggage, or inner demons, holding us back.

My little story makes it sound too easy. Who wouldn't let go of the Mao calendar if it stood in the way of a good marriage? But often our unhealthy attachments lurk just below the waterline of our consciousness; we're not even fully aware that they are working their mischievous magic. We slowly become shackled by old habits, desire for control, the ways we've always done things before, lust, you name it.

Or we become enslaved by our pride, deep fears, peer pressure, or greed. In fact, all those demons seemed to have conspired simultaneously against some of the unhappy young investment bankers I met over the years. They hadn't chosen the profession because the job attracted them and aligned with their sense of what matters. Rather, they had kind of stumbled into banking because all the high achievers on campus were competing for those well-paying jobs. Their inner demons—peer pressure, fears of being an outsider, a touch of greed, and a prideful drive to be one of those few who landed a job offer from a prestigious bank—had basically been in charge of the decision-making process.

That's how it works: Our inner demons flex their dark power at the worst possible moments, when we're on the verge of major decisions about relationships, jobs, or serious moral dilemmas. We want our best selves to be making those decisions, focused only on what matters—that is, our sense of mission and higher purpose in life.

Instead, if we're not careful, those inner demons end up subtly pulling the strings. We don't notice while we're in the throes of the decision; we realize only a couple years later, when, for example, we look back and wonder how we plunged headlong into that terrible relationship or were vain enough to waste so much money on that diamond-crusted, warthog-leather handbag.

A short anecdote will illustrate a particular kind of unfreedom that can derail us at major turning points.

Early in my investment-banking career, I was shocked to hear of a manager berating a talented subordinate with these words: *Take more risk!* The employee had been hesitant to trust his judgment, and the manager knew that no one succeeds without the guts to take prudent risk when appropriate.

Up to that moment, risk had been a bad word for me. Parents and teachers warned against taking risks; risks resulted in skinned knees, school detentions, and visits to hospital emergency rooms. "Take more risk" was the mantra of the pitchfork-wielding devil on my left shoulder, while the white-shrouded angel atop my other shoulder steered hard in the opposite direction.

Well, allow me to be the angel who tells you that you will never become your best self without taking some risk. You will risk failure with every marriage proposal, job change, relocation to a new city, or choice of one college major over another. Even when the odds of failure outweigh those of success, a considered risk may still make sense, as every successful entrepreneur, artist, and author knows. Only when you are willing to risk failure are you able to "risk success."

For that very reason, school can sometimes be a poor preparation for life. When one does enough homework, the right answer on the multiple-choice test is usually clear. But with relationship, career, and business decisions, the right choice is rarely so certain, no matter how much homework has preceded it. Ironically, the smartest folks sometimes end up the worst decision makers simply because they're afraid of making choices unless the right answer is clearly apparent.

Often it's not. A mentor once told me that the best thing to happen in his career was botching his first major decision. The *best* thing? Yes, he said. Life went on, he picked himself up, and he learned that most mistakes aren't fatal (unless, of course, you're a pilot, a surgeon, and so on). Life frequently offers second and third chances—not always chances to undo past mistakes but chances to do good nonetheless.

So, from that time, he was never afraid to make a decision. He modeled the proactive, world-embracing attitude that characterizes good leaders.

Your life, too, will be choice filled. I wish I could say that as long as you have a clear sense of what matters, you will easily discern and do what matters. Alas, life is not that easy. The values that matter to you should remain constant over a lifetime, like a guiding north star. But your circumstances, resources, and virtually everything else in this volatile world will keep changing around you. Through all that, you'll remain pointed toward your true north only by making choices.

Your fragile humanity will complicate all those choices. The true-north part of you may be attracted toward one job, but your greedy inner demon may steer hard toward a different one. Or your current boss may offer a challenging "stretch" assignment, and your best self may see it as a wonderful growth opportunity, but a fearful inner demon, loathing the risk of failure, may hold you back from accepting the demanding new role.

Only when you are free from whatever internal baggage misdirects you will you be free for full pursuit of what ultimately matters. Only the author willing to risk reputational ridicule will create a groundbreaking new novel. Only the graduate who is free from the peer pressure to follow the herd of classmates into some faddish profession, for example, can entertain the job offer that resonates more deeply with her sense of purpose.

Everyone has friends who made lousy job choices, or married the wrong person, or married the right person but then wandered into destructive affairs. How can you do better than that? Whenever you face a major decision, dig deep within yourself and look for the demons—the unfreedoms, the unhealthy attachments—that want to make the decision for you. Drag those demons from their subconscious lairs into the disinfecting daylight. Your envy, greed, or fears are less likely to drive a decision once you become fully conscious of their potential influence.

Once you've banished the demons, you're free. You're free to make a choice guided only by the important questions: What matters here, and which choice will make me proud of the life I'm leading?

Make It Personal

Think of some decision you made within the past few years that might have been too driven by some inner demon or unfreedom. What lesson can you take away from that for your future choices?

Can you experiment this coming week, in some small way, with freeing yourself from some "unhealthy attachment" to become freer for the journey? Focus especially on inner unfreedoms, such as fear that prevents you from trying something or an unhealthy attachment to social media.

Habit 6—Change Your Little Part of the World

Motivational speakers pump up audiences with feel-good bromides like, "You can change the world! Yes, you!"

My motivational advice? Forget that nonsense. You're not going to change the world.

But you can change some miniscule corner of it, and that will be plenty.

I learned that lesson on "Magic Mountain," as I now call it. Why "Magic"? Well, if you owned a gold mine, your investment would become worthless once the mine was depleted. But what if the mine's treasures never ran out and were replenished daily? Sounds like magic, right?

I visited Magic Mountain quite some time ago. It was swarming with prospectors who had paid authorities for the chance to harvest the mountain's treasures. But don't picture prospectors in miners' helmets. Instead, these prospectors worked in T-shirts, shorts, and flip-flops.

They weren't mining gold. They were mining garbage.

Magic Mountain is a sprawling garbage dump that stretches as far as the eye can see on the outskirts of Manila, the Philippines. Metro Manila is composed of some thirteen million people, and thirteen million people generate a whole lot of trash, and lots of it has ended up on this dump. Impoverished prospectors used to pay for the right to scamper up the garbage hillside. They would overturn layer upon layer of Manila's refuse and scavenge plastic, metals, or other valuables, all in the hope of earning back their up-front investment and a few pennies more by selling their harvest to middlemen.

Every few minutes, another garbage truck would rumble up Magic Mountain and tip its mother lode onto the pile. Enterprising pickers would crowd in close to each dump truck, as if ducking under a waterfall. To my eyes, it was a trash fall of every rotten leftover ever thrown in a garbage pail; to theirs, it was a cascade of money. The most valuable trash was invariably snapped up as soon as it hit the pile, and some Magic Mountain prospectors therefore paid more to stand extra close beside the unloading trucks.

Young children also scampered across Magic Mountain. Shorter and nimbler than their parents, the children stooped to comb through garbage without suffering the back weariness that afflicted impoverished adult trash prospectors. Some of the children seemed to enjoy it, much as wealthier children enjoy backyard scavenger hunts at birthday parties.

I had been invited to Magic Mountain to witness human resilience amidst dreadful, unjust circumstances. So I was surprised to find a small house with a wading pool at the base of this giant mound of trash. A vacation property? In that godforsaken place? Its proprietors turned out to be two nuns who minded young children every afternoon. The kids may have been wonderful garbage pickers, but little children grow hungry and cranky after working in temperatures that hover around 100 degrees Fahrenheit. The nuns took the children off their parents' hands each afternoon, fed them, played games, and taught them to read.

And the wading pool? No child likes to wash, whether he or she lives in luxury or beside Magic Mountain. But every child likes to splash around on a hot day. The sisters installed the wading pool to trick the children into bathing.

I had been prepared for Magic Mountain's smell but not for its sheer scale, the steam rising from the stinking pile, or the stinging in my eyes. Nor had I imagined discovering that nursery school, which seemed tiny and hopeless against that mountainous backdrop. I was more bothered by the reek of despair than that of refuse. This can't be the way humans are supposed to live, by God's plan or anyone else's.

And the sisters' meager efforts seemed futile against the monstrous array of challenges faced by this community of the city's poor: unemployment, severe inequality, environmental degradation, substance abuse—you name it. No effort of theirs would heal what plagued Magic Mountain.

Indeed, not enough has changed in the years since my visit. Authorities have now outlawed scavenging at Magic Mountain's summit. But garbage pickers still work the dump's outskirts. Neither those sisters nor anyone else has cured the social ills that bedevil that place.

But those sisters never imagined that they would end homelessness, poverty, or our planet's other injustices. Instead, their calculus was more straightforward: *Will we wait for a perfect solution, or will we do something now?*

They call to mind the story of a man strolling along a beach. He happens upon a young child, who is rescuing starfish that have been stranded by the receding tide. The kid picks up a starfish, walks down to the surf, and gently places the starfish into the water. Then he repeats the process.

"Hey, kid," the man says, "look around. There must be a thousand starfish stranded on this beach. You think you're going to save them all?"

"No," replies the kid, picking up another starfish, "but I'm going to save this one."

If that story is too cloying for you, consider Charles B., who worked at Chattanooga's Memorial Healthcare System, cleaning and polishing its floors, meticulously guiding his buffing machine in graceful arcs up and down the length of a lobby floor. How many people pass through a busy hospital lobby each day? A few hundred? And how many of them really notice workers like Charles, or what they do? A few, if any.

After all, hospital visitors are worrying about a loved one's recovery from heart surgery or their own cancer diagnosis. And Charles wasn't curing cancer. But he wasn't demotivated. He once described his job this way: "I'm grateful to have a ministry that touches lives as I shine floors."

Really? Yes. One day, a hospital visitor told her husband that the lobby floors "have a shine where you can see yourself. I can see the bottom of my feet as I walk across them, and it reminds me of Christ walking on water." The woman later complimented Charles's boss, who passed the word back to him. Lots of us wonder whether our work makes any difference in others' lives. Yet "just" by shining floors, Charles managed to free someone, at least momentarily, from anxiety and stress over an illness.

Whether we are cleaning up floors, data in spreadsheets, babies' bottoms, or legal disputes, work is transformed when we manage to perceive it as Charles did: It's a *ministry* (the word's root means "service") to fellow humans.

Charles knew he wasn't healing the world, any more than those Magic Mountain sisters thought they were ending poverty. Don't wait for the golden, world-changing opportunity; extract gold from the opportunity at hand.

As what's popularly known as the "Archbishop Oscar Romero prayer" puts it: "We cannot do everything and there is a sense of liberation in realizing that. This enables us to do something, and to do it very well. It may be incomplete, but it is a beginning, a step along the way, an opportunity for the Lord's grace to enter and do the rest."

Mother Teresa thought likewise: "We cannot do great things on this earth; we can only do little things with great love."

Don't worry about saving every starfish or righting all the world's injustices. Do something with love for someone today. Be grateful that you can make a small difference.

Make It Personal

Is there a "Magic Mountain" in your life: a place of great injustice and need where you can make some difference?

What small, positive difference could you make in someone's life tomorrow?

Habit 7—Keep Walking up the Hill and down the Hill: Persevere

Keep going. Seriously, just keep going.

I first met Sr. Saturnina during a speaking trip to Venezuela. I had flown there from New York in a few hours. She, in contrast, had first journeyed there decades earlier on a weeks-long odyssey by car, train, bus, and ship.

That got her only as far as downtown Caracas; then she kept going, first by bus to where the buses stopped at the end of the paved roads, and from there by foot. Caracas is rimmed by lush hills that eventually blend into the Andes, hills that are beautiful to behold but torturous to climb. Imagine doing so, as Saturnina and her colleagues did, in old-fashioned nuns' habits on steamy summer days in this land not far from the equator.

But walk they did—up the hill and down the hill, one hour of walking each way, two hours of walking each day. In those days, that district, named Petare, had no schools, no roads, no running water, and not much else that we associate with civilization.

But plenty of poor Venezuelan children lived there, and Saturnina began by herding some 250 of them into an open-air shed with a tin roof. She taught reading and writing, stopping each day when about an hour of daylight remained so that she could walk back down through rutted fields without twisting an ankle. Each morning, the cycle began anew: up the hill and down the hill.

Much changed in the decades after Saturnina's arrival. The sisters eventually built a little convent in which to live among those they served. Eventually, their pupils, some of Latin America's poorest children, studied not in shacks but in clean classrooms. The school started providing a daily hot meal for each student, and those with fevers could visit a small clinic that Saturnina opened. Paved (if potholed) roads eventually snaked through Petare, so visitors no longer had to clamber uphill on foot.

Still, I wondered whether Saturnina had complicated feelings toward the end of her life, when she traveled those paved roads and pondered her life's work. Yes, no longer did anyone twist ankles in barren, rutted fields, but only because no open spaces remained on that hillside: ramshackle dwellings had been constructed haphazardly in every spare nook of this slum, each newly completed roof of scavenged scrap becoming the foundation for an even more ramshackle dwelling that teetered atop it.

One can scarcely believe that the stack of cards remained standing. Sometimes, it didn't. Even today, when heavy rains fall, so occasionally do some of the houses in a landslide that brutally culls Petare's impoverished population before new arrivals assume their places.

And, to be frank, Saturnina's school began serving hot meals only because it had to: Children who didn't get a decent meal at home sometimes fainted in class. And the bright classrooms? An antidote to the windowless homes the children returned to, where single parents, overwhelmed by poverty's challenges or beset by substance-abuse problems, couldn't or wouldn't offer the nurturing love that every child deserves.

Saturnina left her family and native land and invested some seven decades in this place; yet, at first blush, the community ended up worse off than when she started. Her perseverance intrigued me. Petare seemed to have been sliding downhill for all those decades that Saturnina was walking uphill, yet she kept going.

I asked her how she did it. She was a religious person, so I wasn't surprised that she framed her answer accordingly: "The kingdom of God," she replied, "*se hace presente*—it's coming alive; it's making itself present; it's here."

Huh? In that chaos? That impoverished barrio didn't look like a kingdom to me. But I was looking at substandard houses, sewage, and other things; she, in contrast, looked at people and saw a more just world inching closer with every loving gesture that helped kids "live with the dignity that corresponds to children of God's kingdom."

It didn't matter that reality fell far short of her vision; she seemed a happy warrior, energized by a battle that had captured her heart. "It's what I've been working for from my very first day here until today. . . . It's something I've been fighting for, struggling for."

Psychologists have discovered that human resilience, the capacity to persevere, is like an emotional muscle. That is, we build stronger resilience through the right "exercises," particularly these three: showing gratitude, being altruistic, and exhibiting a strong sense of life purpose. No wonder, then, that Saturnina could scamper up and down those hills, year after year, setbacks and disappointments notwithstanding:

She had hit the resilience trifecta as a happy warrior whose strong sense of mission sprang from her altruistic desire to serve.

She died not long ago, and as I recalled her life story, I could almost hear this book's chapters snap neatly together. Do you want to make today matter? If so, you will need to persevere. Some of your plans won't work out; people will disappoint you; you'll disappoint yourself. You'll transcend setbacks only by building your resilience, by learning to put one foot in front of the other, up the hills and down the hills of your life journey.

You'll build the needed resilience by acquiring the habits championed throughout these pages: living for a purpose that matters greatly to you, for example, and becoming an altruistic person dedicated to giving away your sneakers, and being grateful always.

In good times, this "virtuous circle" of mutually reinforcing habits will make life feel like riding a bicycle on level ground: Momentum keeps building, and each crank of the pedal comes more easily than the previous one.

And on life's bad, uphill days? Your good habits will generate the fierce willpower needed just to stay on the bike, to keep going.

One of Saturnina's colleagues, Sr. Marisel Mujica, remembered how Saturnina "never saw the obstacles, only the opportunity." That's why Petare's real story is not about challenge but about resilience in the face of challenge. "We see many who are fighting," Marisel told me, "to lead a dignified life and to get their families ahead. We see parents who don't eat so that their children can eat. They don't surrender. That's the character of the people in this neighborhood. That fight is inspiring."

Keep going.

I recall a moment during the three-hundred-mile walking trek I once made along Spain's famous Camino de Santiago. At the end of one long day, some two dozen of us sweaty, bedraggled pilgrims gathered in a west-of-nowhere rural church. The priest read a boilerplate prayer for our safety, then closed his prayer book and improvised: "I know you are hot and tired. But keep going. If you are looking for answers, you will find answers. If you are looking for peace, you will find peace. If you are looking for God, God will find you."

We appreciated his hopeful promise because, frankly, most of us didn't feel peaceful after another scorching day under Spain's unforgiving sun. We just felt hot and tired. Yet we persevered in walking toward our goal, just as Saturnina, her

Petare neighbors, and so many of you persevere toward what matters.

I think of so many who remain dedicated to jobs or causes even when they are not rewarded fairly, can't see results, are overlooked, are taken advantage of, or find no encouragement. The most courageous among us may be all those who simply manage to keep going, even though they don't feel very courageous at all.

How do all these people find the strength to do what they do? "Be bold, and mighty forces will come to your aid," a nineteenth-century pastor once said. We associate "boldness" with battlefield heroics or with putting a man on the moon.

But surely it's boldness enough to act justly when life has treated us unfairly, or to remain committed to excellence when it isn't recognized. I believe that, as these everyday heroes struggle through trying and often unjust circumstances, mighty forces are coming to their aid.

What are those mighty forces? I believe, like that priest in Spain, that "if you are looking for God, God will find you," that even as we are looking, and even when we mostly feel lost, God is somehow finding us, whether or not it feels that way. When we set ourselves toward some worthy purpose that transcends our meager strength, we tap into a source of meaning, peace, and courage that is beyond us. That certainly seemed to happen for Saturnina.

I know that you sometimes feel hot and tired and can't be bothered. But keep going. Persevere. Up the hills and down the hills of your journey. The writer Mary Anne Radmacher once put it this way: "Courage doesn't always roar. Sometimes courage is the little voice at the end of the day that says I will try again tomorrow." Amen to that.

Make It Personal

Think of the moment when you showed your greatest resilience and perseverance. What strengthened you to keep going?

Altruism, gratitude, and a clear sense of life purpose can help build emotional resilience. Which of these three qualities is a strength of yours? Which do you need to develop further?

Habit 8—Be More Grateful

Gratitude is like cholera.

Both are highly contagious, potent, and spread person to person. But where cholera induces death, gratitude induces happiness, as I discovered while delivering a leadership workshop for school principals. I told them about a completely unanticipated e-mail from my boss one morning, thanking me for my good efforts on a project.

I probably read that e-mail ten times during the following days. I would endure a run-in with corporate bureaucrats or a frustrating encounter with a whiny coworker, then retreat to my office, reread that e-mail, smile to myself, pull my corporate helmet back on, and get back into the game. Remember an earlier chapter's story about mutinous, sullen bankers on bonus day? Well, my boss probably got more motivational mileage out of that short e-mail than from the bonus check he handed me that year. (But, let's be honest, I still wanted the bonus.)

Anyway, a few hours after I recounted this story at the school principals conference, one attendee approached me. Her assistant principal had discovered and resolved a problem at school and e-mailed his update to her, and she had dashed off a succinct reply: "I agree with how you handled it."

Then the principal looked at me, smiled shyly, and continued in a charming Southern drawl: "But then I remembered that story you told us—about showing gratitude? So, I sent another e-mail, thanking my assistant principal for his dedication to the school." She yanked out her smartphone and showed me the assistant principal's response: "Thank you so much for saying that. You made my day."

Well, by now the beaming principal looked about ready to cry, and I suddenly felt like I was going to cry, even as I was thinking, *I don't even know these people.* Gratitude will do that—in your family, work group, or community. Catch people doing something right, as management guru Ken Blanchard puts it, and thank them for it.

But let's backtrack. Those are stories from the advanced class—Gratitude 201: Express Gratitude to Others. Let's start with Gratitude 101: Be Grateful for All You Have. If there's a recipe for making today matter, gratitude is the "secret sauce," and science proves me right. In a famous experiment, researchers contrasted what we'll call a "gratitude group" and a "grouchy group." The first group's members regularly jotted down moments or people for which they felt grateful; the grouches journaled about what irritated them.

After a month, the gratitude group were more optimistic, felt better about their lives, exercised more, and made fewer doctor visits than the grouchy group. How much money have Americans spent on self-improvement schemes in pursuit of those very same outcomes? Dr. Lowney's prescription is this: Invest $1.99 in a pad and pen, then take the miracle drug every night. Write down three reasons you're grateful.

I remember my mother's long recovery from an auto accident. She was wheelchair-bound for weeks, struggling to recover her strength and mobility. One afternoon, I watched a physical therapist roll the wheelchair between a set of parallel bars, lock the wheels, and crouch down: "Mrs. Lowney, I want you to push yourself out of the wheelchair with both hands, and stand up, and grab these bars to support yourself. Okay?"

Doubt crossed my mother's face. She raised herself a few inches, then dropped back down. But it was further than she'd gotten in futile attempts over the previous two weeks, and her face now changed from worry to concentration. She gathered herself for a second effort.

And up she went. She stood up out of the chair the way a few billion of us do every day. She stood unsteadily for a few seconds and looked around, taking in the world from a perspective she hadn't had for more than two months. Then she slumped back down, exhausted. She exhaled with relief and satisfaction and gave the therapist a weak high five.

As my mother's legs strengthened, my eyes opened to a miraculous world. Near my apartment building are six flights of concrete stairs that I had skittered down every day of my commuting life, thinking about work or the weather or a thousand things other than my footfalls. But during her recovery, I did think about my footsteps. Once or twice, I walked down those same stairs slowly and gratefully, savoring the marvel that I could walk at all. I tried to imagine what impossibly coordinated symphony of bone, joint, and muscle took place with each step.

A friend with aged, infirm parents brought an equal marvel to my attention: She was struck by wonder one morning that from a standing position she could bend over, remain balanced, and tie her shoes.

We take so much for granted. Premature babies who would have been given up for dead a century ago are now nursed to a healthy infancy. We Americans enjoy nearly twice the average life expectancy of our great-grandparents and immeasurably higher living standards. Twice as many of us graduate from high school as did then; almost all of us are literate. We choose from among countless occupations and pastimes.

Today's average American lives more comfortably than the nineteenth century's wealthiest tycoons, who never beheld the sky from an airplane seat, browsed a website, heated soup in a microwave, or looked at a color photograph.

As I think of all I have and all I have been given, I'm certain of this much: I haven't been grateful enough—and, chances are, neither have you. Be grateful now, tomorrow, every morning, and every evening. Gratitude will make you happier, and, just as important, will energize you to struggle on behalf of your marginalized brothers and sisters across the planet, billions of whom still lack their just share in the miracles of progress I've just described.

The problem is, we forget. Yeah, I have so much, but life is still stressful: I miss a train or spill coffee on my pants; my kid throws up at school, and my phone battery dies while I'm stuck on hold with the insurance company. When such things happen, forget gratitude—enroll me in the "grouchy group." I become "a feverish, selfish little clod of ailments and grievances complaining that the world will not devote itself to making [me] happy," as George Bernard Shaw so memorably put it.

Don't let it happen. Don't let yourself become a feverish, selfish little clod. Remain grateful for all you have, and you'll be blessed with a "whole life" in an era when countless Americans feel stuck with split lives. They may feel deeply aware of God's presence when praying, walking on a beach, or spending time with old friends. Then they return to work, and God disappears. They relapse into de-energizing, split-life thinking: Work is work, spirituality is spirituality, and the two have nothing to do with each other.

Many of us feel pulled in so many directions that we no longer feel whole, almost as if we're slowly disintegrating. In fact, that's exactly what's happening. We're not literally falling to pieces, but whenever we can't connect spirit to body or faith to work, we really are "dis-integrating," because the root of the word *integrate* means "whole."

This book's habits map a path back to wholeness, by reintegrating our spirituality throughout our everyday actions. Gratitude is a perfect example; it's intrinsic to all the world's great spiritual traditions. Christians are exhorted to "rejoice always, pray without ceasing, give thanks in all circumstances," and Jews are encouraged to "Give thanks to the Lord, for he is good, for his steadfast love endures forever." We're healing a broken part of ourselves, our disintegration, simply by becoming more grateful—not to mention all those other payoffs identified by the psychologists who studied the "gratitude group" and the "grouchy group." Science is vindicating the wisdom of Roman orator Cicero, who proclaimed that "gratitude is not only the greatest of all virtues, but the parent of all the others."

But forget about all those other payoffs for a moment: Be grateful just because you have so much to be grateful for.

Make It Personal

What are three things you are grateful for right now?

For whom are you grateful? Before continuing to the next chapter, why not call or send them a note to tell them why you're grateful for their presence in your life?

Habit 9—Control the Controllables:
Listen to the Still, Small Voice

Can you imagine some idiot who lived with a saint and never bothered getting to know the guy? I'm that idiot.

The saint or, rather, saint-to-be is Walter Ciszek, whose candidacy for sainthood is steadily churning its way through the Vatican bureaucracy. When I was a Jesuit seminarian, I lived for a time in the same hundred-person Jesuit community where Fr. Ciszek ate dinner.

He typically sat at one of the side tables in the community's large dining room. I would move through the buffet line, scan the tables, and invariably bypass Ciszek to sit elsewhere. Why? Ciszek was polite but quiet; I was twenty-three and wanted to mingle with livelier colleagues.

That says something encouraging about the self-effacing style of saints and something discouraging about me. In fact, it's even worse than it sounds so far, because I knew of Ciszek's remarkable life story, yet regularly passed up the chance to learn more. He had journeyed to Soviet Russia as a missionary and soon after was arrested. The secret police didn't take kindly to a freelance Catholic priest roaming their atheist realm. Ciszek was falsely accused of spying for the Vatican and subsequently endured two decades in Soviet gulags and Siberian work camps.

He passed day after day in a tiny cell that was, as he later wrote, "about seven by twelve feet, with grimy stone walls and one little window high in the wall. The room was always dark." But that wasn't the worst part: That seven-by-twelve cell was home to a dozen people. "At night, we all huddled together on the rough-hewn benches to sleep. If someone turned over in his sleep, he was liable to wake the whole crowd."

Imagine days with nothing to look forward to besides the next interrogation or the next meager meal. Compounding the physical privations was the frustration that things hadn't worked out according to Ciszek's plans. He went to Russia to *do* things, such as minister to heroic believers who struggled to keep faith alive in underground churches. How endlessly demoralizing to sit in prison and stew bitterly over enforced idleness. He was accomplishing none of those ambitious plans he had hatched on God's behalf.

But an epiphany dawned. "God's will was not hidden somewhere 'out there'" in those grand plans Ciszek had concocted. Rather, he began to see his situation as God's "will for me. What [God] wanted was for me to accept these situations as from his hands, to let go of the reins and place myself entirely at his disposal." Ciszek came to understand that our first calling is the one that we so often overlook: to find meaning and grace where we are right now.

We often obsess over the job we wish we had or what we could have been doing if our luck had been better. Such preoccupations distract us from the opportunity that lies right in front of us, whether it is to be a better friend or father this evening or even only to sit in a jail cell, pray, think good thoughts, and treat our captors with civility and kindness.

Ciszek's story is not about giving up and shrugging with a resigned "Whatever." Rather, his story is about "controlling the controllables." Healthy individuals focus their energies where they can exert positive influence; they don't squander energy in fruitless lament over what they cannot control or change.

For example, I think of my father, who, to better his prospects, immigrated to the United States from an impoverished island off Ireland's coast, worked hard, and supported a family. Then, at a relatively young age, an unexpected cancer diagnosis precipitated his nine-month slide to death. Instead of providing for his family, he found himself relying on that family to bathe, shave, and feed him. At life's end, he could control only his attitude: whether to find meaning in suffering and die with dignity or to stew in bitter resentment at the unfairness of it all. He chose well.

He had controlled the controllables throughout his life, embracing the chances that came his way, bearing the risks and uncertainties of emigrating in pursuit of a better life. Yet, faced with a cancer diagnosis, he manifested humble, graceful acceptance of all that he couldn't control.

Both he and Ciszek embodied the prayer often associated with Alcoholics Anonymous: "God, grant me the serenity to accept the things I cannot change, the courage to change the things I can, and the wisdom to know the difference."

For example, we cannot venture back in time to undo some injustice inflicted by an unfaithful spouse or an unscrupulous manager. Our only way to assert control is by letting go of the long-nursed anger and pain that remain from such unhappy episodes. Likewise, serenity is essential when I don't enjoy the robust health I long for or must hang on to an unfulfilling job to support my family responsibly.

But courage is imperative if I can pursue alternatives such as enhancing that job or leaving it entirely. The courageous take initiative wherever they can. They develop their gifts and talents, fight against the world's injustices, and try to make the world better. Yet, at the same time, they recognize how much lies beyond their control, even as the rest of us go nuts trying to bend the world to our will.

Those two attitudes—bold action and serene acceptance—appear incompatible. One quality involves fierce will: I will seize the opportunities I'm given. The other entails humility: I'm not master of this universe; it's God's world, not mine; I can't make it spin around me.

Those two qualities do seem damn near incompatible with each other. And, yes, I'm challenging you to cultivate both. The key to doing so comes in the Serenity Prayer's final phrase: "the wisdom to know the difference."

Wisdom sounds a bit fuzzy, an antiquated notion that has been supplanted by technology and science. Well, a search engine may help you craft a résumé or research wedding caterers, but it won't tell you whether it's time to change jobs or whether this person is the one to marry. For those questions, the Old Testament psalm has it right: "Happy are those who find wisdom. . . . She is more precious than jewels, and nothing you desire can compare with her."

Pray for the wisdom to be a great decision maker at life's turning points, because you'll have to make far more choices than that psalmist did three thousand years ago, or even than your great-grandparents did a century ago. For centuries, most of our ancestors would typically follow a parent's livelihood, pursue that same work for a lifetime, live and die in the town of their birth, and embrace their family's religious beliefs and moral code.

Now? Many of today's college graduates will switch jobs ten times before age thirty and move ten times in a lifetime. Whole industries will blossom and die during their working lives. Young adults don't reflexively embrace their parents' religion; they consciously choose whether to follow a religious tradition at all. That's a whole lot of decisions, even before one decides which of forty cereal brands to buy or which of a hundred cable channels to watch.

While it's easy to find apps offering shopping and entertainment advice for superficial decisions, where can a person find the wisdom app for life's serious choices?

Ciszek found the wisdom app. But he had an advantage that you and I lack: enforced solitude. Imprisoned with nothing, certainly without modern-day conveniences such as smartphones or music players, Ciszek was left to tune in to his own inner voice. Which is really hard to hear. Forget all the biblical drama about burning bushes, voices in your head, and angelic messengers. Maybe that happens once in a billion lifetimes. For the rest of us? Ignatius of Loyola, the founder of the Jesuits, wrote that the inner voice of spiritual wisdom comes "gently, lightly . . . like a drop of water going into a sponge."

Ignatius was echoing the Bible's Elijah, who witnessed a "great wind, so strong that it was splitting mountains and breaking rocks in pieces." But Elijah perceived that "the LORD was not in the wind" or in the earthquake or fires that followed. Rather, Elijah found God in the "sheer silence" that came afterward. As another translation puts it, Elijah heard God's "still small voice."

The Quaker minister Parker Palmer said that *calling*, a deep sense of what we are meant to do and become, "does not come from a voice 'out there' calling me to become something I am not. It comes from a voice 'in here' calling me to be the person I was born to be."

No wonder we're all stressed and confused. We make countless more decisions than our ancestors did, yet we make them amidst a cacophonous world that drowns out the "still small voice" inside us. And we make it hard on ourselves: Tethered to technology, we're tuned in to distractions and external stimuli but out of touch with what's far more important: that still, small inner voice and what it might be whispering right now. When we tap into that, we tap into the wisdom to discern what we can control and what we cannot.

I can't explain why God didn't wire us with more user-friendly wisdom apps that would make it easy to perceive the right choice at life's turning points. My smartphone can give me turn-by-turn directions from my Bronx apartment to Keokuk, Iowa; why didn't God make it similarly easy for me to discern whether I should take this job or that one?

Don't worry: There is a wisdom app, one requiring nothing more than the commitment to daily practice. "Pulling Together All Ten Habits" will explain how to download the wisdom app into our hearts and minds.

Make It Personal

Recall a situation in which you did poorly at "controlling the controllables"—that is, you shied from showing the needed courageous initiative; or, you should have shown more peaceful acceptance of a situation beyond your control. What do these episodes teach you about yourself?

Call to mind one or two major decisions that you are likely to face within the coming years; pray for the wisdom to handle those situations well.

Habit 10—Answer This Hurting World's Call for Happy Warriors

Bob's leadership story and yours are different in only one important way, as I'll explain.

Shortly after retiring as a onetime managing partner of a global accounting firm, Bob was strolling down Manhattan's Fifth Avenue one day. A thirty-something guy in a suit suddenly veered toward him, smiled broadly, and stuck out his hand: "Bob! I can't believe I'm running into you. I've always wanted to thank you. Remember that meeting with such-and-such client, when I was a junior accountant? They were pressuring us to sign off on an accounting approach that verged on unethical, and it was tense. But I can still picture how you calmly convinced them why you couldn't sign off on what they wanted to do. Ever since that day, I've tried to model myself on how you handled that episode."

Bob tells me that story, pauses, smiles, and shares his punch line: "You know something, Chris? I didn't remember that guy, and I didn't remember that meeting!"

Here's the only important difference between Bob's story and yours: He was lucky enough to find out how profoundly he had influenced someone he scarcely remembered. Chances are, you've influenced others similarly. You just haven't had the serendipitous encounter to confirm it.

I'm not talking about your abiding influence on a spouse or close friends, though, of course, that's paramount. I mean the other thousand people you've encountered in random moments as a soup-kitchen volunteer or in kindness shown to a junior colleague, a fearful patient, a confused student, or a discouraged neighbor. As the poet Gerard Manley Hopkins put it, "For Christ plays in ten thousand places, / Lovely in limbs, and lovely in eyes not his." You, too, have sometimes been those eyes and limbs.

I've no doubt about it, simply because I've been surprised to learn when I myself have said or written something that helped someone else at a key moment. Believe me, it's not because I'm dispensing nuggets of incomparably brilliant wisdom. Rather, my ordinary words or actions happened along at an extraordinarily opportune moment in someone else's life. Is that grace—God's hand playing through our hands, eyes, and voices? We will find out someday. For now, just ponder this: Perhaps it's destined to happen in some passing encounter of yours today.

You're making every day count more than you think, in the impacts you're having.

I can't introduce you to everyone you have touched, but I'd wager that poet Nikki Giovanni's verse applies to you: "We're better than we think we are, but not as good as we can be."

Everyone needs confidence for the journey ahead, and the first half of Giovanni's axiom can help: You're better than you think you are. You're good, first of all, because your dignity is your birthright. You don't need to earn or prove it, nor can anyone take it from you. And if you've never doubted that because you've been loved and supported as befits your dignity, then lay aside this book for a minute and e-mail a thank-you to parents, teachers, neighbors, or friends who nurtured you.

But if you haven't been treated as befits a child of God, then the previous chapter's Serenity Prayer may help. You could not control the misdeeds of guardians or others, nor can you wander back to change your history. Pray for serenity and, perhaps, for a generous spirit of mercy toward those who failed you.

My friend Jim Keenan, a Jesuit theologian, speaks of mercy as "the willingness to enter into the chaos of another to answer them in their need." If that's so, then we all need mercy, because chaos trickles into everyone's life now and then. In fact, some of us have surfed tidal waves of chaos for years. Even so, none of us is as bad as the worst thing we've ever done. We're valuable not because of what we accomplish or how well we cope; we are valuable simply because we exist.

This book has been deepening our self-awareness. We've pondered what matters and taken stock of our talents, fears, unhealthy attachments, and reasons for gratitude.

Self-reflection will surely make you a better leader, but it can hammer your self-esteem along the way. Self-knowledge invariably brings awareness of how ill prepared we have been for some of life's challenges. For example, the nurse didn't present a handbook for your screaming newborn, nor were you equipped to cope with your teenager's substance-abuse problem nor when your job required feats of imagination and patience as you tried to manage-without-managing a dysfunctional supervisor. In all those circumstances, and hundreds more like them, we feel inadequate to the task and become our own worst critics.

That's why Bob's story is worth remembering. Yes, we screw up sometimes, but we are having more positive influence than we think. We're all showing leadership, which we defined as "pointing out a way or direction and influencing others toward it." We're living that definition every day in classrooms, on playing fields, at work, and at home. By our example, we are implicitly pointing a way forward: "Hey, look: This is the way human beings ought to live; these are the values we should model." Remember Giovanni's axiom: "We're better than we think we are."

That said, this book is not a self-esteem manual, and I'm not handing out trophies. So instead of a pat on the back right now, let me offer a supportive kick in the ass. I hope that the first part of Giovanni's axiom inspires you to do something about its second part: "We're better than we think we are, but not as good as we can be."

Our hurting world is plagued by challenges that can't be overcome unless we bring big heart and our best selves to confront the world's ills. You didn't ask for that burden and opportunity, but you're here on the playing field at this moment in history, and that's how "calling" often emerges in life. Sometimes you get to choose your moments, causes, and vocation. But, other times, you don't get to choose the opportunity. The moment chooses you: A troubled colleague or student walks into your office; a loved one takes ill; a refugee family is resettled in the neighborhood; a natural disaster befalls your hometown; or politicians float proposals that would unjustly disadvantage the community's poor or marginalized.

Righting the world's injustices is a grueling struggle that won't end in our lifetimes. But remember Saturnina? That happy warrior fought for a more just world, day after day and year after year, as she went up the hill and down the hill, "not seeing the obstacles but seeing only the opportunity."

We need a few million more happy warriors like her. And the world needs you to be one of them. It's time to step up and lead. Bring big heart. Then remind yourself of Bob's serendipitous encounter with his former subordinate, and trust that you, too, are having more impact than you probably imagine.

Make It Personal

Who has influenced you for the better but remains unaware of it? Why not call or e-mail that person to tell him/her?

Think of a couple of unanticipated chances that you have had over the years to have some positive influence on someone else's life.

Pulling Together All Ten Habits:
The Wisdom App

Was yesterday successful, and how do you know?

Most of us could only answer such questions superficially: "Yes, I got through most of my to-do list."

But we're aiming for something higher than that: to make today matter. We want to hold ourselves accountable to that high standard, and this chapter will equip us to do so. To learn how, please journey with me to London's John Carpenter Street, where J. P. Morgan's European headquarters sits.

I walked that narrow street awhile ago, swung around the corner, headed uphill on Dorset Rise, and ducked into the easy-to-miss alleyway that leads to St. Bride's church. I hadn't been there in years but remembered everything, including what was no longer there, perhaps torn out during a renovation: the back corner pew where I must have sat a couple hundred times during my London working days.

My habit seldom varied. I would finish lunch, stroll to St. Bride's, sit for a few minutes in the deserted church, and then return to the maelstrom of e-mails, phone calls, meetings, and crises.

Funny, only during that recent visit did I realize what I had been doing in that church all those years ago. I had thought I was just taking a break, enjoying the simple chance to "be" without the pressure to "do." But something else was going on, I now see. I was subconsciously reinventing a practice that I had learned decades earlier, during my time as a Jesuit seminarian, long before I ever imagined that my journey would include John Carpenter Street.

Granted, *Jesuit* and *investment banker* don't sit easily in the same frame. One is a "helping others" profession, while the other is sometimes regarded as a "help yourself" profession.

But in one respect, the Jesuit founder, Ignatius of Loyola, had to solve the same human problem that today's investment bankers have to solve, the same problem that nurses, homemakers, students, teachers, and the rest of us must solve: how to remain mindful of what matters while reeling through each day's distractions.

When the Jesuits were founded, most religious orders relied on a monastic regimen to keep members on track, at peace, and focused. Multiple times each day, all the monks would gather for communal prayer. If Brother Baker had been daydreaming all morning or annoyed at Brother Gardener, that prayerful interlude might have gotten Baker back on track.

But Ignatius had envisioned an activist religious order, its culture later epitomized in phrases such as "living with one foot raised" and "contemplatives in action." His Jesuits would be too fully immersed in their ministries to gather multiple times daily for communal prayer, as monks did.

Still, while we can dispense with a regimen like retreating to chapel each day, we can't dispense with the need to stay focused and recollected as we bob along on a tide of e-mails, phone calls, tasks, texts, and meetings. How do I remain centered when life pulls me in every direction? How can I stay recollected when I'm always on the run? How do I focus on what matters when I'm too distracted to think at all?

Ignatius saw those challenges in the sixteenth century, and modernity's intense pace has, since then, exacerbated every one of them. The fallout is obvious: We're history's most advanced civilization, yet we're saddled with mounting levels of stress, depression, anxiety, and alienation.

We're ignoring this worsening challenge. Credit Ignatius with tackling it head-on by crafting a simple regimen, which Jesuits call an *examen* in their fondness for arcane Latin terminology. I'll call it a "mental pit stop." Jesuits will howl at that colloquialism, not to mention the oversimplified version of the process that follows. But I want to render it accessible to tech workers, teachers, and office managers who haven't been studying Jesuit spirituality. And I want to enable those of any (or no) religious tradition to tap its wisdom.

So, here's a simple version of the practice: Take two five-minute breaks each day, once after lunch and again at day's end. Make it a real break: no music, social media, television, or phone calls during these minutes. Take a few deep breaths, or say a prayer, to calm and clear your mind. Then contemplate three things in turn.

1. Remind yourself why you're grateful.

2. "Lift your horizon." That is, don't focus six inches ahead, at the next e-mail to answer or the next errand to do. Instead, focus on the big picture. Call to mind what ultimately matters to you, your sense of purpose, or your most important life goals this year. Then,

3. Relive the past few hours. What was going on inside you? What can you learn from these past hours that might benefit your next few hours? For example, if you

were upset all morning, why? If you snapped at a colleague or your spouse and need to make amends, resolve to do so.

That's it. Now, get back into the game. Make the most of the next few hours, then refresh yourself with another mental pit stop later.

An irony struck me as I strolled along the London business district near St. Bride's that afternoon, each street lined with sophisticated financial institutions, every office boasting all the budget-busting, cutting-edge technology a financier could desire: technology for analyzing stock prices, calculating risks, executing trades, video conferencing, you name it.

Only one technology was missing: the costless yet priceless technology I just described—the wisdom app, the habit of daily reflection. It's priceless because it matters not how exquisitely programmed one's computer systems may be if malfunctioning humans then handle the output.

Let me illustrate the point through a life-and-death anecdote shared by renowned Harvard Medical School professor Dr. Jerome Groopman. In *How Doctors Think*, he recalled a patient "with seemingly endless complaints whose voice sounded to me like a nail scratching a blackboard." One can imagine how a hypochondriac could test the patience of an overworked caregiver.

After listening to one such complaint and rapidly diagnosing minor gastric trouble, Groopman prescribed antacids. He blithely ignored the patient's protests that the problem was persisting—until he was paged to the emergency room a few hours later to find the woman dying of a heart aneurysm.

That's a rough story to tell about oneself. We can give Groopman credit for having the guts and humility to tell it, because he wanted to share his painful lesson learned that afternoon: "Emotion can blur a doctor's ability to listen and think. Physicians who dislike their patients" are prone to cut them off, ignore their complaints, or cling to unduly hasty judgments just to avoid the unpleasantness of dealing with them.

This Harvard Medical School doctor could access the world's most sophisticated diagnostic technology, but that didn't help him, because he didn't access vital data about himself: *What's going on inside me now? Am I in the proper state of mind to encounter this patient without letting my emotions or biases warp my judgments?*

Most of us don't make life-and-death diagnoses as Groopman does, but all of us deal with family members, colleagues, or others who annoy or irritate us. We can't just pay attention to external data like a doctor's lab reports, the office revenue figures, or my kid's report card. We must attend equally to our internal data, the emotions, fears, or other inner demons that impede our effectiveness or impair our judgment as we react to what's happening at any given time. Each mental pit stop will help us to do just that.

The genius of this daily practice is not its sophistication but its intuitive simplicity. In fact, I constantly hear about practices that yield similar benefits. Consider an acquaintance's nightly dinner-table routine. Each family member talks about some "proud of" moment, recounting something that went well at home, school, or work. Through their "proud ofs," this family reflects on the day and expresses gratitude for what transpired.

Then there is the New York City taxi driver who dangles Muslim prayer beads from the cab's rearview mirror. When a driver cuts him off, he instinctively reaches for the beads. That simple gesture wards off anger and calms him down.

And if taxi driving in New York seems hectic, imagine bus drivers in Jakarta, Indonesia, a city roughly three times more populous than New York yet lacking a subway system. Imagine piloting a bus through Jakarta's rush-hour snarls. A bus driver there concocted his own accountability practice. He put a small box on his dashboard into which he deposited a penny whenever anger or foul thoughts welled up within him.

The technique worked: He placed forty-nine pennies into the box on the first day of his practice but only sixteen a week later. This small act renewed his peace of mind and helped him stay focused on what really matters. He was making his life whole by connecting his work to his spiritual beliefs about how one ought to live.

If you're attracted to that prospect of weaving your spirituality more tightly into your days, why not transform each mental pit stop into a moment of explicitly spiritual reflection? For example, take the same five-minute break described earlier and structure it as follows:

1. Step back from the day's chaos and recall that you are in the presence of God or your understanding of a Higher Power.

2. Pray for enlightenment and wisdom.

3. Be grateful! You have so much; don't take it for granted.

4. Mentally revisit the past few hours to draw lessons learned from the day so far. Pay attention to what you have been thinking and feeling, not just to what you've been doing. Consider how God may have been present to you in the events and conversations that have unfolded. Rabbi Lawrence Kushner once defined holiness as "being aware that you are in the presence of God." That's not just when you sit in church or temple

but wherever you are, whoever you're with, and whatever you are doing.

5. Be honest with yourself. If you've not upheld the values you profess, acknowledge that.

Finish with hopeful resolution for the future. Be thankful for the opportunity to have recollected and reoriented yourself as necessary. Then, put the past behind you and create a better future by living the words of St. Paul: "Forgetting what lies behind and straining forward to what lies ahead, I press on toward the goal."

Even as your examen reaps insights from your past to improve your future, above all it will pull you into mindful, grateful awareness of this present moment. Our days typically unfurl in frenzied preoccupation with errands, meetings to attend, and phone calls to return. The Buddhist monk Thich Nhat Hanh pointed out that we humans often focus on to-do lists and future plans, "but we have difficulty remembering that we are alive in the present moment, the only moment there is for us to be alive."

I promised to teach a technique that would almost magically incorporate all ten of the habits outlined in this book, and the wisdom app does just that. Do your daily examen, and your checklist for making today matter will complete itself. Gratitude? Check. Remind myself what matters?

Check. Come to grips with any unhealthy attachments that led me astray today? Evaluated whether I used my talents well? Seized any opportunity to give away my sneakers? Check, check, check.

What's more, you'll be holding yourself accountable to your highest standards of what a meaningful life entails. You will be defining success on your own terms by asking yourself, *Am I becoming the person I most want to be?* You will avoid the trap of letting social media, popular culture, or the neighbors define success for you.

Too many folks get sucked into that unwinnable rat race. They start living "outside in," so to speak, surrendering control of their self-esteem to what others say or think of them: *If others admire me, I guess things are going well; if they don't admire me, something must be wrong with me.*

The examen articulates the opposite, an "inside out" approach to life whereby you decide what a meaningful life entails and become accountable to your own standards.

Despite all those benefits, the examen doesn't happen on its own. Doing it daily requires commitment and consistency. There's no way around it. You have to practice this practice. It's too easy to slack off and neglect it. I speak from experience, because I often get caught up in each day's distractions and neglect it myself. Case in point: I can vividly recall a drive or two into New York's LaGuardia Airport, where my mind was ping-ponging with traveler's preoccupations—*Will I be on time, have I packed what's needed, and are the arrangements in order at my destination?*

LaGuardia's mazelike ramp network used to skirt a large parking lot where some hundred or more idle taxis would wait to pick up passengers. At certain times of day, I might see a knot of Muslim cabbies at the parking lot's perimeter, their prayer rugs spread across the greasy pavement. They somehow ignored diesel fumes, racing engines, and bleating horns. They briefly stopped worrying whether they would earn enough today to pay tomorrow's rent. Instead, they prostrated themselves, touching their foreheads to the ground in reverence to God.

That gesture reminded them what ultimately matters in their lives, and seeing them at prayer would remind me what matters in mine. I would momentarily forget my own worries. I, too, would pray. I would recall that I had neglected to take my own prayerful pit stop and would resolve to do better tomorrow.

On some tomorrows I do better, but on many tomorrows I don't. No matter. Every day still brings another chance. New opportunities dawn, and new challenges arise. As I make my way through them, I try to learn from my past, live in my present, and look forward to my future.

Make It Personal

Identify two five-minute blocks of time each day during which you could do a practice like the examen.

Do you use other spiritual practices to remind you daily of what matters?

Twenty-Four Brand-New Hours

"Writing is like driving at night in the fog. You can see only as far as your headlights, but you can make the whole trip that way."

E. L. Doctorow was describing the novelist's craft. If that's what writing fiction feels like, try living reality. After all, authors are gods of their fictional worlds, free to redo unpleasant chapters and edit away the heartache. They can invent happier endings and slide first drafts into the recycle bin. Nothing lost, save time and effort.

Would that the do-overs came so easily in real life. We don't have as much control over our lives as an artist might have over his work. We sometimes suffer: Career plans fail, children take ill, or recessions happen. At our worst moments, we may stare into the metaphorical fog and wonder what comes next. Can you foresee the next ten years of your life clearly? Only if you're deluding yourself. The next ten months? Maybe, if you inhabit a more stable world than I do.

Still, Doctorow's message is hopeful, not gloomy. And my experience has borne him out. You can't see your whole future clearly, "but you can make the whole trip that way." Focus on the challenges and opportunities in front of you, and you will get there. By cultivating the right attitudes and habits, you will author more of your story than you imagine. Not every job or relationship will unfold as you wish, but you are the author of what matters most: how you behave, react to life's vicissitudes, and treat others along the way.

As an eighteen-year-old, I imagined that my high-beam headlights were illuminating a straight path through life and all the way to my deathbed: I entered a novitiate that year, fully expecting to end my days as a Jesuit priest. Then life happened. I discerned that my calling in the world lay outside the Jesuits. Since then, I've been an investment banker, hospital-system board chair, author, social entrepreneur, and husband. I've lived on three continents and spent chunks of time on two more. I foresaw none of those transitions five years before they happened; in a couple of cases, I saw those transitions coming only on the day a boss dropped them into my lap.

At first, it was frustrating. I wanted to grip the steering wheel more assertively and drive my own future, to decide where to go and the fastest route to get there. My seeming inability to control my future felt as unsettling as night fog. I wondered where the detours and occasional wrong turn would take me.

You know how I eventually found greater peace while looking ahead? I learned to look back. Peering ahead at the fog and twisty roads still leaves me queasy sometimes. But looking into my rearview mirror? Hmm. Consoling. That problem that once loomed ahead like an impassable road-block? I got through it. And that year when I seemed to be zigzagging or going in circles? Now I see that I was indeed getting somewhere as a person and learning as I went. Being assigned to work in Japan when I had little desire even to visit the place? Turned out to be about the best work experience in my banking career. Each passing year further convinces me that the philosopher Kierkegaard had it right: "Life can only be understood backwards, but it must be lived forwards."

Each stage of the journey has somehow prepared me for some stage further along the path. And a constellation of people helped me along the way. Some are old friends who have accompanied me for decades; others popped up in my life at a crucial moment and made some vital difference before our paths diverged and we headed separate ways.

Have all those encounters and experiences been mere coincidence? Do I delude myself when I find some providential pattern here?

As the psalmist put it, this world is "too great for my understanding." I'm humbled by its immensity and complexity. I don't pretend to understand it all. But I can say this: The uncertainties, setbacks, and turns haven't left me frightened of what's ahead. Instead, I've become a more trusting, confident traveler. I believe a benign providence is at work, even if I can't prove that to you, and even if it doesn't seem that way when life occasionally feels like a night journey on a twisty road, with a broken GPS and a gas tank near empty.

That's why I ask you to make this book about your next twenty-four hours rather than your next twenty-four years. Live the next day well, then the one after that, and in time, you'll be looking in the rearview mirror at a life lived well.

I'm not advising you to wing it through life, twenty-four hours at a time. We need to plan responsibly about career, retirement savings, children's education, and so on. But life never unfolds exactly according to our blueprints. The main benefit of all that planning is simply that it spurs the first steps forward. After that, you'll be resourceful enough to figure out what steps should come after.

And, all the while, you'll be learning, developing skills, and building resilience, and you will grow in confidence as you overcome obstacles and uncover new opportunities. In short, you'll become wiser—provided that you start with the ultimate end in mind: You want to head toward what matters, so first confirm what matters to you in life, the kind of person you want to become.

Then, take stock of your journey so far. If you've mostly been heading the right way, give thanks and bring big heart as you keep going.

But if you've not been the person you want to be, then reorient yourself toward true north and change course. It's never too late to bend the curve of your life trajectory.

In any case, start now. Make the most of the next day by living in the spirit described by Thich Nhat Hanh: "Every morning, when we wake up, we have twenty-four brand-new hours to live. What a precious gift! We have the capacity to live in a way that these twenty-four hours will bring peace, joy, and happiness to ourselves and others."

That's easier said than done. Modern life is complex, massively scaled, and fast changing. We humans are innately weak, needy, prone to distraction, and easily tempted off course. Marry our frailty to the vexing environment in which we live and work, and even focusing on the next twenty-four hours can be challenging.

So, don't try to do it all by yourself. Help others along the way, and let them help you. An African proverb puts it this way: If you want to go faster, go alone; if you want to go farther, go in a group. Yes, you can move faster alone—until you're the one who needs direction, help, or accompaniment. You can move faster alone, but where to exactly? To live in this world is to be in relationship with others. To lead is to influence others, and we influence others only after winning their respect, confidence, and trust.

No solitary heroes trudged through previous chapters. Rather, all our heroes were in relationship with others. I introduced you to teachers, coaches, managers, mentors, parents, and healers, among others. I encouraged you to "give away your sneakers" by seizing each day's opportunity to help someone in need. Don't reach the end of your journey weighted down by a lifetime of missed chances, all those sneakers that you never gave away, so to speak.

Finally, no epic journey succeeds without courage and commitment. Faced with the complex human predicament, some people end up drifting passively on the tide of events. Others try to take charge where they can. This book is for those who want to show leadership by engaging the world proactively and by thinking hard about what matters most.

An earlier chapter recounted the old fisherman's prayer: "Oh God, thy sea is so vast and my boat is so small." So it is. Some days are sunny, others stormy, and still others downright terrifying, when the maelstrom engulfs you and you fear capsizing. All this will make you humble before the world, teaching you to appreciate your limits, because the winds are beyond your control and some voyages are too risky to undertake.

Still, seafarers don't spend their whole lives tied up in port. Every boat is made for sailing, and so is yours. Don't be shackled by your fears.

I remember when South African freedom fighter Nelson Mandela emerged after enduring twenty-seven years in prison. I was astounded by the man's courage and grace; it seemed so effortless, as if he drew from a deep well of natural gifts.

But then he set me straight. I later read an interview in which he confessed, "My greatest enemy was not those who put or kept me in prison. It was myself. I was afraid to be who I am."

Well, everyone's afraid. And no one has enough self-confidence. Don't let your fears steal your opportunities.

Contribute where you can. A hurting world sorely needs you, so start your journey to more proactive leadership. Your confidence will rise every time you get knocked down and pull yourself back up again, with each obstacle you overcome, and with every discovery that inspires you to explore what lies around the next corner.

Make today matter.

Acknowledgments

This book is immeasurably better thanks to those who helped in numerous ways. I wish to acknowledge a few of them by name, begging the pardon of some whose names may slip my mind.

First, thanks to Joe Durepos, who first conceived the idea for this book, championed it within Loyola Press, and offered patient guidance while shepherding it to publication. I thank those who edited it under great time pressure, including Vinita Wright, who has been a friend and partner for many years and a few books. Thanks as well to Susan Taylor for a conscientious copy edit. Likewise, thanks to the marketing team, including Andrew Yankech and Becca Russo; Becca has long been a responsive, supportive partner in making books available at talks or in other venues.

Louis Kim, Katherine Lawrence, Angelika Mendes-Lowney, and Christian Talbot all read an early draft and offered helpful feedback.

The book is built upon the stories of many folks who are "making today matter." I thank all of them for the values they model. I refer to a few of them in the text only by their first names, in a couple of cases to protect their privacy. The text includes, in quotes, snippets of conversation; all such conversations took place, and I am confident that I accurately convey their substance; but I don't claim to remember, with word-for-word accuracy, conversations that in some cases took place many years ago, and will beg the reader's indulgence that I have used quotes in these cases.

One of the stories concerns Steve Duffy, who taught me at Regis High School; it's a great joy that my nephew Colin now attends the same school. May ours be the noble heart, Colin.

Whether I had good days or bad days of writing, I knew I could count on my wife, Angelika, to be a constant, loving supporter.

All of these people made the book far better than it would have been otherwise. Many inadequacies remain, for which I alone am accountable.

Endnotes

Page 1: *If, like archers*, Aristotle, *Nicomachean Ethics*, trans. Terence Irwin (Indianapolis: Hackett, 1985), 1.2.

Page 2: *If one does not know* Seneca the Younger, quoted in Henry Ehrlich, *The Wiley Book of Business Quotations* (New York: John Wiley & Sons, 1998), 190.

Page 4: *To give as much love* adapted by author, after reading an anecdote in Steve Martin, "The Death of My Father," *New Yorker*, June 17, 2002, 84.

Page 4: *Whatever you did* Adaptation of Matt. 25:40.

Page 4: *What does the Lord* Mic. 6:8.

Page 4: *Do to no one* Tob. 4:15.

Page 4: *Spread love everywhere* Attributed to Mother Teresa.

Page 6: *For I do not do what I want* Rom. 7:15.

Page 11: *I see myself radiating Christ* Steven V. Duffy in *Regis Alumni News* (Spring, 2005): 14.

Page 12: *it is not so much their subjects* Frederick Buechner, *Now and Then* (New York: Harper & Row, 1983), 12.

Page 17: *I will suggest a means* Attributed to Augustine, accessed October 30, 2017, https://catholicsaints.info/saint-augustine-of-hippo/.

Page 17: *Whatever your hand finds* Eccles. 9:10.

Page 18: *If you plan on being anything less* Variations of this quote are attributed to Abraham M. Maslow; see, for example, Joan Neehall-Davidson, *Perfecting Your Private Practice* (Bloomington, IN: Trafford, 2004), 95.

Page 25: *They are either sullen* Roy C. Smith (former Goldman Sachs partner), quoted in "The Chatter," *New York Times*, January 2, 2005.

Page 28: *person earning $50,000* David Whitman, *The Optimism Gap: The I'm OK—They're Not Syndrome and the Myth of American Decline* (New York: Walker and Company, 1998), 145n22.

Page 32: *One night in June* Ginger Smith, "An Emergency Department Story," *Sacred Stories*, 9th ed. (Denver: Catholic Health Initiatives, 2008), 89.

Page 50: *We cannot do everything* The prayer is often attributed to Blessed Oscar Romero (+1980) but in fact was composed by Bishop Ken Untener in 1979. Accessed October 30, 2017, http://www.usccb.org/prayer-and-worship/prayers-and-devotions/prayers/archbishop_romero_prayer.cfm.

Page 50: *We cannot do great things* Attributed to Mother Teresa but considered to be a paraphrase by the Mother Teresa of Calcutta Center. Accessed October 30, 2017, http://www.motherteresa.org/08_info/Quotesf.html.

Page 59: *Be bold, and mighty forces* This is a popularized adaptation of a quote from Basil King, *The Conquest of Fear* (New York: Garden City Publishing, 1921), 29.

Page 60: *Courage doesn't always roar* Bobi Seredich, *Courage Does Not Always Roar: Ordinary Women with Extraordinary Courage* (Naperville, IL: Simple Truths, 2010), foreword: Mary Anne Radmacher.

Page 62: *Catch people doing something right* Kenneth H. Blanchard, *Catch People Doing Something Right: Ken Blanchard on Empowerment* (Provo, UT: Executive Excellence Publishing: 1999).

Page 66: *feverish, selfish little clod* Lewis Casson, Introduction to George Bernard Shaw, *Man and Superman: A Comedy and a Philosophy* (New York: The Heritage Press, 1962), xxv.

Page 66: *Rejoice always, pray without ceasing* 1 Thess. 5:16–18.

Page 67: *Give thanks to the LORD* Ps. 118:29.

Page 70: *about seven by twelve feet* Walter J. Ciszek, SJ, with Daniel L. Flaherty, SJ, *With God in Russia* (New York: McGraw-Hill, 1964), 61.

Page 71: *God's will was not hidden* Walter J. Ciszek, SJ, with Daniel L. Flaherty, SJ, *He Leadeth Me* (New York: Image Books, 1975), 88.

Page 73: *Happy are those who find wisdom* Prov. 3:13–15.

Page 75: George E. Ganss, SJ, *The Spiritual Exercises of Saint Ignatius: A Translation and Commentary by George E. Ganss, SJ* (Chicago: Loyola Press, 1992), #335.

Page 75: *great wind, so strong* 1 Kings 19:11–12.

Page 75: *does not come from a voice* Parker Palmer, *Let Your Life Speak: Listening for the Voice of Vocation* (San Francisco: Jossey-Bass, 2000), 10.

Page 78: *For Christ plays* Gerard Manley Hopkins, SJ, "As Kingfishers Catch Fire," in Norman H. Mackenzie, ed., *The Poetical Works of Gerard Manley Hopkins* (Oxford, UK: Clarendon Press, 1990), 141.

Page 79: *We're better than we think* Nikki Giovanni, "We Are Virginia Tech," Virginia Tech Convocation, Blacksburg, Virginia, April 17, 2007. Used by permission of Nikki Giovanni.

Page 80: *the willingness to enter into the chaos* James F. Keenan, SJ, *The Works of Mercy: The Heart of Catholicism* (New York: Rowman & Littlefield, 2005), xiii.

Page 87: (Boston: Houghton Mifflin, 2007), 24.

Page 88: *Emotion can blur* Ibid, 25.

Page 91: *Forgetting what lies behind* Phil. 3:13–14.

Page 91: *but we have difficulty remembering* Thich Nhat Hanh, *Peace Is Every Step: The Path of Mindfulness in Everyday Life* (New York: Bantam, 1991), 5.

Page 95: *Writing is like driving at night* George Plimpton, ed., *Writers at Work 08: The Paris Review Interviews* (New York: Penguin, 1988). Accessed October 30, 2017, https://en.wikiquote.org/wiki/ E._L._Doctorow.

Page 97: *Life can only be understood backwards* Søren Kierkegaard, Journals IV A 164 (1843). Accessed October 30, 2017, https://en.wikiquote.org/wiki/S%C3%B8ren_Kierkegaard.

Page 98: *Too great for my understanding* Adapted from Ps. 139:6.

Page 99: *Every morning, when we wake up* Thich Nhat Hanh, *Peace Is Every Step*, 5.

Page 101: *My greatest enemy was not those* Attributed to Nelson Mandela.

About the Author

Chris Lowney, a former Jesuit seminarian, served as a Managing Director at J. P. Morgan & Co. on three continents. He currently chairs the board of CHI, one of the nation's largest healthcare systems. Author of the best sellers *Heroic Leadership* and *Pope Francis: Why He Leads the Way He Leads*, he speaks widely on leadership and has been featured in *Forbes*, the *Harvard Business Review*, and the *Wall Street Journal*, among others. One hundred percent of Chris's proceeds from *Make Today Matter* will be donated to charities that support education for underprivileged communities. Visit chrislowney.com to learn more.